Business German
Parallel Text
Short Stories
English - German

Learn Business German

Learning Business German with parallel text is the most rewarding and effective method to learn a language. Existing vocabulary is refreshed, while new vocabulary is instantly put into practice. Our stories evolve around business making the terms and phrases easier to remember in the learning process.

Learning Business German with Parallel Text Recommended for beginners with a good basis of German-, intermediate level learners and as a refreshers course. The stories have been written to keep the readers attention and are fun to read for you to learn through your motivation.

Table of Contents

PARALLEL TEXT

Anfangsschwierigkeiten
Growing Pains

Ich bin am Montagmorgen früh aufgewacht, mit einem Knoten im Bauch so groß wie meine Faust.
I woke up early Monday morning with a knot in my stomach as big as my fist.

Wenn es einen Tag gab, der sich als der erste Tag vom Rest meines Lebens qualifizierte, dann war es dieser.
If any day in my life was going to qualify as the first day of the rest of my life, this would be it.

Mein einziger Geschäftspartner und ich hatten später an diesem Tag einen Termin mit einem **Angel Investor** um unseren **Businessplan** zu besprechen.
*My only business partner and I were scheduled to meet with an **angel investor** later in the day to discuss our **business plan**.*

Ich saß am Fenster und für einen kurzen Moment blitzten mir tausend Dinge durch den Kopf.
I sat at the window and for a brief moment a thousand things flashed through my mind.

6

Doch wenn ich den nächsten Schritt machen wollte, musste ich mich konzentrieren.
But if I was to move to the next step I needed to focus.

Ich nahm einen großen Schluck kalten Kaffee und wandte mich wieder der bevorstehenden Angelegenheit zu.
I took a long drink of cold coffee and returned to the matter at hand.

Jedes Unternehmen, **das etwas wert ist**, beginnt mit einer Idee.
*Any business **worth its salt** begins with an idea.*

Nach der Idee beginnt die harte Arbeit.
After the idea, the hard work begins.

Die harte Arbeit führt dann zu einem **in sich geschlossenen Businessplan**.
*The hard work then translates into a **tight cohesive business plan**.*

Mein **Geschäftspartner** Jim Bowles und ich hatten fast zwei Jahre lang an unserer **Geschäftsidee** gearbeitet.
*My **business associate** Jim Bowles and I had worked on our **business idea** for almost two years.*

Wie viele unserer Generation waren wir mit

einem gesunden Respekt vor der Umwelt aufgewachsen.

Like many of our generation we had grown up with a healthy respect for the environment.

Im Licht unserer guten Erziehung und eines ausgesprochen **sozialen Gewissens** haben wir unsere Fähigkeiten und Energie zusammengerafft und sind in den Bereich der grünen Technologien vorgedrungen.

*In light of our good upbringing and a decidedly **social conscience** we gathered our skills and energy and pushed forward into the field of green technology.*

Unsere Idee und Schwerpunkt waren Biokunststoffe.

Our idea and area of focus was Bioplastics.

Mein Name ist Lannie Parker. Gemeinsam haben wir PARKER & BOWLES Bioplastics gegründet.

My name was Lannie Parker. Together we founded PARKER & BOWLES Bioplastics.

Biokunststoffe waren aus unserer Sicht mehr als nur eine **trendige Offenbarung**, die sich irgendein Umweltspinner ausgedacht hatte.

*Bioplastics in our view was more than just a **trendy epiphany** imagined by some tree hugger.*

Sie ergaben **geschäftlich einen Sinn**.
*It made good **business sense**.*

Kunststoffe, als **Baumaterial**, hatten sich zu einem der wichtigsten Materialien in der **verarbeitenden Industrie** entwickelt.
*Plastics, as a building material, had become one of the **primary materials** used in the **manufacturing sector**.*

Weil Kunststoff ein Produkt auf Erdölbasis war, bedeutete das, dass ein großer Anteil der **Unternehmenswelt**, die Kunststoffe verwendet, vom Öl abhängig war; in Nordamerika und Europa bedeutete das oft, dass man von ausländischen **Exporten** abhängig war.
*Because plastic was a petroleum based product that meant a huge portion of the **entrepreneurial** world using plastics was dependent on oil; in North America and Europe that often meant relying on foreign **exports**.*

Zu verändern, wie wir Kunststoffe herstellen und natürliches pflanzliches Material zu verwenden, um die Herstellung neu zu formulieren, würde eine Spielwende von monumentalen Ausmaßen bedeuten.
*Changing how we made plastic and using natural plant based material to reformulate its manufacture would be a **game changer** of monumental proportions.*

Mit Hilfe von Fetten und Stärken aus Pflanzen Kunststoff herzustellen würde eine ungesunde Abhängigkeit vom Öl beenden, die der Industrie helfen würde zahllose Dollars in der Herstellung zu sparen.

Using the fats and starches from plants to make plastic would end an unhealthy dependence on oil, which would help industry save countless manufacturing dollars.

Pflanzen zu benutzen um Kunststoffe herzustellen bedeutete, dass die Industrie sich vollkommen **erneuerbarer Ressourcen bedienen konnte** und dass das dazu führen würde, dass die Industrie das tun kann, was sie am liebsten tut... und das war Geld zu machen.

*Using plants to make plastic meant industry would be **tapping into** a totally **renewable resource** and that would allow industry to do what it enjoys best ... that was making money.*

Unser Job heute war es, unseren **Angel Investor** davon zu überzeugen, dass unsere Geschäftsidee **vernünftig und tragfähig war.**

*Our job today was to convince our **angel investor** that our business idea was both **sound and viable.***

Unser **Businessplan** war die formelle Dokumentation unserer Geschäftsziele, wie sie erreichbar waren und der **spezifischen Pläne,**

die wir anwenden wollten, um sie zu erreichen.
*Our **business plan** would be a formal documentation of our business goals, how they were attainable and the **specific plans** we intended on using to reach them.*

Wenn wir unsere Hausaufgaben gemacht hatten, würde unsere Geschäftsidee die dringend benötigten Dollars unseres **potentiellen Investors** für uns gewinnen.
*If we had done our homework our business idea would attract the much-needed dollars from our **potential investor**.*

Als wir schließlich den **Angel Investor** später an diesem Tag getroffen haben, waren wir überrascht, ihn zu kennen.
*When we finally met the **angel investor** later that day we were surprised to see that we recognised him.*

Der Angel Investor war ein ortsansässiger Geschäftsmann im Ruhestand, der im Alleingang zwei Baumärkte in der Region zu **blühenden** und erfolgreichen Unternehmen aufgebaut hatte.
*The angel investor was a local retired businessman who had singlehandedly built two building supply stores in the area into a **thriving** and successful business venture.*

In der Tat so gut, dass ein riesiges Kaufhaus,

das in der Region Einzug gehalten hatte, dem ortsansässigen Unternehmer klugerweise ein **lukratives Angebot** gemacht und sein **Unternehmen aufgekauft hatte**.

*So well, in fact, that a huge box store moving into the area had wisely made a **lucrative offer** to the local business owner and subsequently **bought him out**.*

Als er anfing, unseren Businessplan durchzulesen, erinnerte er meinen Partner und mich daran, dass jegliches Investment, das er in unser Unternehmen machen würde, im Austausch für **Wandelschuldverschreibungen** oder eine **Beteiligung am Eigenkapital** geschehen würde.

*When he began to read through our business plan, he reminded my partner and I that any investments he might make in our company would be in exchange for **convertible debt** or **ownership equity**.*

Jim und ich sahen uns nervös an, während der ältere Herr seine Brille auf die Nasenspitze schob und mit ernster Miene weiter unsere Unterlagen überflog.

Both Jim and I looked nervously at one another while the older gentleman propped his glasses on the tip of his nose and proceeded to scan our paperwork with a serious look on his face.

Die erste Komponente des Businessplans war die **Kurzfassung**.
*The first component of the business plan was the **Executive Summary**.*

Was diesen Punkt anbelangte, fühlten wir uns sicher.
We felt confident at this point.

Jim Bowles hatte in der Stadt in einer High-Tech Computer-Firma ein paar Jahre lang in einer Management-Funktion gearbeitet, bis das **finanzielle Fiasko** 2008 sie in den **Konkurs** getrieben hat.
*Jim Bowles had been involved in a high tech computer company in the city in a management capacity for a good number of years or at least until the **financial fiasco** of 2008 drove it into **bankruptcy.***

Sein eigentlicher akademischer Hintergrund war jedoch in der Chemie.
His actual academic background though was as a chemist.

Was mich betrifft, ich war der Betreiber/ Eigentümer eines landwirtschaftlichen **Zulieferunternehmens** und hatte an der Uni im Hauptfach Betriebswirtschaft studiert.
*As for myself, I had been the operator owner of an agricultural **supply company** and a business major while in university.*

Wir beobachteten, wie unser Angel Investor mit dem Finger über das Papier zur nächsten Überschrift wanderte.

We watched as our angel investor ran his finger down the paper to the next heading.

Die war **Kundenanalyse**.
*It was **Customer Analysis**.*

Wir mussten beide im Stillen diesen Teil des Plans in unseren Köpfen durchgegangen sein, denn ein selbstbewusstes Lächeln machte sich auf unseren Gesichtern breit.

We both must have been silently reviewing that portion of the plan in our heads at the very same time because a confident smile filled our faces.

Kunststoff war ein **etablierter** Baustoff.
*Plastic was an **established** building material.*

Wenn wir ihn billiger und umweltfreundlicher herstellen konnten als erdölbasierten Kunststoff indem wir ihn biologisch abbaubar machten, dann wäre er ein **Selbstläufer**.

*If we could make it cheaper than petroleum based plastic and more environmentally friendly through biodegrading then it would be a **no brainer**.*

Alles würde auf einen guten, soliden **Umsatz** hinauslaufen.

*It would add up to good solid **revenue**.*

Der letzte Teil des Businessplans war die **Wettbewerbsanalyse**.
*The last portion of the business plan was the **Competitive Analysis**.*

Welche Art von Unternehmen waren bereits auf dem Markt, die man als **Wettbewerb** betrachten konnte?
*What kind of businesses already existed in the marketplace that would be considered **competition**?*

Welche Fähigkeiten und Dienstleistungen unterschieden unser Unternehmen von den anderen und zeichneten uns in den Augen der **Verbraucher** aus?
*What skills and services would make our company different and make us stand out in the eyes of **consumers?***

Angesichts der Art des Unternehmens und seiner grünen Technologie waren wir sicher, dass unsere Konkurrenz **dünn gesät war**.
*Regarding the nature of the business and its green technology we felt confident our competitors were **few and far between**.*

Es war eine relativ neue Technologie, und wir waren davon überzeugt in einen **Markt einzutreten**, der noch in den **Kinderschuhen**

steckte.
*It was a relatively new technology and we felt we were **entering the market in its infancy**.*

Es würde Kämpfe geben, doch mit Entschlossenheit hofften wird, uns den Hindernissen stellen und tragbare Lösungen für jedes vorstellbare Problem finden zu können.
There would be struggles, but with determination we hoped we could face the obstacles and find solid solutions to any perceivable problem.

Nach langer Überlegung sprach der Angel Investor schließlich.
The angel investor finally spoke after a long deliberation.

Er war mit dem Lesen des Businessplans fertig.
He had finished reading the business plan.

Er stellte alle relevanten Fragen. Seine Antwort war positiv.
He asked all the pertinent questions. His response was favourable.

Er würde uns ein Investitionsangebot machen, unter der Voraussetzung einer **Due Diligence Prüfung**.
*He would make us an offer of investment, but conditional on **due diligence**.*

Wir waren beide begeistert.
We were both ecstatic.

Das war nur der erste Schritt, doch wir waren auf einem guten Weg.
It was only the first step but we were well on our way.

Ein Unternehmen war im Begriff, geboren zu werden.
A business was about to be born.

Ergreifen des Marktes
Capturing the Market

Das Schild von Parker and Bowles Bioplastics sah beeindruckend aus, wie es sanft zwischen zwei großen Pfosten auf dem Rasen vor dem Fabrikkomplex schwang.
The sign for Parker and Bowles Bioplastics looked impressive as it swung gently between two large posts on the front lawn of the factory complex.

Lannie Parker, einer der **Eigentümer**, die die Firma gegründet hatten, wartete an der Tür.
*Lannie Parker, one of the **founding** owners, was waiting at the door.*

„Guten Morgen Frau Fletcher, freut mich, Sie an Bord zu haben", verkündete Herr Parker, als ich näher kam.
"Good morning Ms. Fletcher, glad to have you onboard," announced Mr. Parker as I drew closer.

„Ich freue mich, hier zu sein", antwortete ich.
"I'm delighted to be here," I responded.

Herr Parker schüttelte mir die Hand und

lächelte.
Mr. Parker exchanged a handshake and a smile.

„Jetzt beginnt der eigentliche Spaß", sagte er.
"Now the real fun begins," he said.

Ich nickte und hätte fast laut gekichert, bevor wir das Gebäude betraten.
I nodded and almost chuckled out loud before entering the building.

Einer Bemerkung stimmte ich nur teilweise zu.
I agreed only partially with his comment.

Es würde Spaß machen, doch es wäre auch eine Herausforderung.
It would be fun but it would also be a challenge.

Die **Vermarktung** einer Idee oder eines Produktes, vor allem, wenn es noch immer neu und von **potentiellen Kunden** ungetestet ist, kann beängstigend sein.
***Marketing** an idea or product, especially when it is still new and untested by **potential customers**, can be daunting.*

Als **Marketing-Beraterin** bin ich von Parker and Bowles Bioplastics beauftragt worden, ihre **Bedürfnisse** in Bezug auf ihr neues Produkt zu bewerten.
*As a **marketing consultant**, I was hired by*

Parker and Bowles Bioplastics to assess their
needs *with respect to their new product.*

Ich würde einen Aktionsplan aus einer Marketing-Perspektive entwickeln und schließlich den Kunden meine Ergebnisse präsentieren.
I would formulate a plan of action from a marketing perspective and eventually present my findings to the client.

Hoffentlich würde ich das Meeting mit den zum Weitermachen erforderlichen Informationen verlassen.
Hopefully I would leave this meeting with the information required to move forward.

Aus den ersten Gesprächen war bereits klar, dass wir zuerst an einem **B2B**-Marketing-Plan arbeiten würden.
*From initial discussions it was already clear that to begin with we would be working on a **B2B** marketing plan.*

Wie bei jedem Plan würde unser erster Schritt sein, die **Vorgaben und Zielsetzungen** herauszuarbeiten und zu priorisieren.
*Our first step, as with any plan would be to highlight and prioritise **goals and objectives**.*

Diese zu definieren war der zentrale Punkt auf der Tagesordnung des heutigen Meetings.
Establishing them would be central on the

agenda in today's meeting.

Ich hatte bereits mit dem Recherche-Prozess begonnen und mein Team hatte ein paar Ideen zusammengetragen, die schließlich zum Entwicklungsprozess der hochwichtigen **Marke der Firma** führen würde.
*I had already begun the research process and my team had been pounding out some ideas that would eventually lead into the process of developing the all-important **company brand.***

Direkt im Anschluss an die Definition der Marke käme der ganze Prozess der Umsetzung erfolgreicher Strategien, um das Parker & Bowles Bioplastic Produkt in eine Reihe verschiedener Branchen einzuführen, von denen einige noch nicht einmal wussten, dass sie das, was diese Firma zu bieten hat, brauchten.
Hard on the heels of establishing the company brand would come the whole process of implementing successful strategies to introduce the Parker & Bowles bioplastic product to a number of different industry sectors; some of which haven't yet woken up to the fact that they need what this company has to offer.

Unser Marketing-Ansatz müsste eine große Bildungskomponente beinhalten.
Our marketing approach would have to include a large educational component.

21

Wir mussten unser **Zielpublikum** über den **Wert** informieren, den dieser innovative Biokunststoff mit sich bringt.
*We needed to let our **target audience** know what **value** this innovative bioplastic could bring to their table.*

Meine Arbeit war mir zugeteilt worden.
My work was cut out for me.

Doch für heute war es wichtig, mit den Kunden zusammenzuarbeiten um all diese wichtigen Vorgaben und Zielsetzungen zu konkretisieren bevor wir irgendetwas in die Wege leiten konnten.
But for today it was important to work with the client to nail down those all important goals and objectives before we could set anything in motion.

Alle mussten der gleichen Meinung sein, um diese Marketingkampagne zu einem Erfolg zu machen.
Everyone would need to be on the same page to make this marketing campaign a success.

Wir wussten dass es eines unserer aktuellen Top-Ziele für Parker and Bowles war, den **Marktanteil** des Unternehmens zu **erhöhen**.
*We knew that one of our current top objectives for Parker and Bowles was to **increase market***

share for this company.

Vor zehn Jahren waren sie unsere Kunden geworden und wir hatten den ursprünglichen Marketing-Plan entwickelt.
It had been ten years since they had become our client and we had developed that initial marketing plan.

Wir sind definitiv ein Teil der Erfolgsgleichung des jungen **Start-up** Unternehmens gewesen, das von dem Hintergrund solider Wissenschaft, ein paar Business Angels sowie einer Menge Hoffnung und Gebete gestützt worden war.
*We had definitely been part of the success equation for what was once a fledgling **start-up** company backed by some solid science, a few angel investors plus a hope and a prayer.*

Ich saß an meinem Schreibtisch, betrachtete die neusten Statistiken und lächelte.
I was sitting at my desk looking over the latest statistics and I was smiling.

Wir hatten erfolgreich eine Krise überstanden und ich war stolz auf die Anstrengungen meines Teams.
We had successfully navigated a crisis and I was proud of my team's effort.

Es gab eine Reihe von neuen Firmen in der Biokunststoff-Branche, die Parker & Bowles dicht auf den Fersen waren und immer mehr traten in den bereits vollen Markt ein.

There were a number of new companies in the bioplastics industry nipping at the heels of Parker & Bowles and more were entering an already crowded market place all the time.

Im letzten **Quartal** hatten wir erstmals einen **Rückgang des Marktanteils** erlebt und wir wussten, dass wir unsere Bemühungen intensivieren mussten, **neue Marktsegmente** zu erschließen.

*Last **quarter** had seen **market share erosion** for the first time and we knew we had to step up our program for developing **new market segments**.*

Der gegenwärtige **CEO** bei Parker & Bowles ist bekannt für seine Fähigkeit, **über den Tellerrand hinauszublicken**.

*The current **CEO** at Parker & Bowles is known for his ability to **think outside the box**.*

Er versteht die Notwendigkeit von Innovation und hat viel in die Entwicklung mehrerer brandneuer Produkte investiert.

He understands the need for innovation and has invested heavily in the development of several brand new products.

Er hat auch mit seinem Team gearbeitet um die Modifikation einiger bereits entwickelter

Produkte zu überwachen.
As well, he has worked with his team to oversee the modification of some already developed products.

Diese Maßnahmen haben das Unternehmen dafür aufgestellt, in einige neue Marktsegmente vorzudringen.
These actions have positioned the company to move into some new market segments

In den vergangenen drei Monaten hatten wir die Möglichkeit, eng mit ihm zusammenzuarbeiten um **Vertriebskanäle** für diese neuen und modifizierten Biokunststoffprodukte zu eröffnen und unsere Bemühungen haben sich deutlich ausgezahlt.
*Over the past three months we were able to work closely with him to open up **channels of distribution** for these new and modified bioplastic products and our efforts were clearly paying off.*

Ich war besonders erfreut über einen der neuen **Broker** mit dem wir in Verbindung mit unserer neusten Marketing-Kampagne zusammengearbeitet hatten.
*I was particularly pleased with one of the new **brokers** we were working with in conjunction with our latest marketing campaign.*

Sie hatte viele Verbindungen in jenen Ländern,

in denen die aktuelle Gesetzgebung die Unternehmen dazu **zwang, sich zu bessern**.
*She had many connections in the countries where current legislation was forcing companies to **clean up their act**.*

Es ist ihr auch gelungen, Verbindungen herzustellen und der **Vermittler** zu sein, der notwendig war, um in diese neuen Märkte **einzudringen**.
*She was able to make connections and be the **intermediary** that was needed to **penetrate** these new markets.*

Das bedeutete, dass sie alle auf biologisch abbaubare Verpackungen für ihre Produkte umstellten.
That meant they were all switching to biodegradable packaging for their products.

Wir waren **noch nicht ganz außer Gefahr** und ich wusste, dass es einige neue Herausforderungen geben würde, doch heute fühlte ich mich optimistisch.
*We hadn't **rounded the corner yet** and I knew there would be some new challenges ahead, but for today I was feeling optimistic.*

Die Dinge lagen besser für Parker & Bowles als im vergangenen Quartal, und ich hatte guten Grund zu glauben, dass wir nächstes Jahr noch mehr Grund zum Feiern haben würden.
Things were better for Parker & Bowles than

they were last quarter and I had good reason to believe there would be even more reason to celebrate next year.

Das Geheimnis unseres Erfolges
The Secret of our Success

Nachdem ich einige interne Berichte von unserer Fertigung gelesen hatte, war ich alles andere als optimistisch was die **Gewinne** im kommenden Jahr anging.
*After reading some internal reports prepared by our production department, I was suddenly feeling less than optimistic about **profits** this coming year.*

Als **CEO** bei Parker and Bowles war ich besonders stolz auf meinen **innovativen Ansatz** in Bezug auf **Marketing-Strategien**.
*As **CEO** at Parker and Bowles I took a special pride in my **innovative approach** to **marketing strategies**.*

Ich hatte eine gute ortsansässige Firma beauftragt, die **Strategien umzusetzen**, und wenn man dem **Finanzbericht** vom letzten Jahr Glauben schenken durfte, dann hatte sich dieser Schritt als Erfolg erwiesen.
*I had hired a good local firm to **implement strategies** and if last year's **financial report** was any indication the move had been a success.*

28

Doch es schien, dass meine Marketing-Strategien nicht ausreichten.
But it appeared my marketing strategies were not enough.

Zahlen lügen nicht und der vorliegende Bericht zeigte, dass die Produktion im letzten Quartal deutlich gesunken war.
The numbers don't lie and the present report indicated production was substantially down in the last quarter.

Anhand der Daten, die ich von meinem Manager erhalten hatte, wusste ich sofort, dass das Problem unsere eigenen **Arbeitskräfte** waren.
*I knew instantly from the data provided by my manager that the problem was our own **labour force**.*

Der Rückgang der **Arbeitsproduktivität** musste gemeinsam mit den Abteilungsleitern der Produktion und dem **Personalmanagement** analysiert werden.
*The decrease in **labour productivity** needed to be **analysed cooperatively** by the production department managers and by **Human Resources management**.*

Ich wollte, dass beide Abteilungen die vorliegenden Daten prüften und so viele Informationen wie möglich in der Fabrik

sammelten.
I wanted both departments to look at the existing data and collect as much information from the actual factory floor.

Sie mussten direkt an die Quelle gehen. Ohne direkten und ehrlichen Input von den Arbeitern selbst wäre jeder Bericht strittig und offensichtlich von zweifelhafter Aussagekraft.
They needed to go directly to the source. Without direct and honest input from the workers themselves, any report would be moot and certainly discredited.

Anfang der folgenden Woche traf ich mich mit den **Abteilungsleitern**, um die Ergebnisse ihres Berichts zu diskutieren.
*I met with **department heads** early the following week to discuss the findings of their report.*

Unsere Arbeitskräfte bei Parker and Bowles setzten sich aus zwei Hauptgruppen zusammen.
Our labour force at Parker and Bowles is comprised of two main labour groups.

Da gibt es die Gruppe der Arbeiter in der Fabrik, die direkt mit unserem Produkt arbeiten, und dann gibt es unser Büropersonal.
There is the labour group on the factory floor that works directly with our product and then

there is our office staff.

Es gibt auch noch eine dritte Gruppe, die in diese Diskussion miteinbezogen werden musste, nämlich die Manager.
There was also a third group that needed to be included in this discussion, namely, the managers.

Es wäre interessant zu sehen, ob die Aufgabe, die ich meinen beiden Abteilungen gegeben habe, auch **Leistungsbewertungen** des Management-Bereichs beinhalten würde.
*It would be interesting to see if the assigned task I gave my two departments would include **performance appraisals** of the management sector, as well.*

Der erste Punkt auf der **Tagesordnung** waren die **Fehlzeiten**.
*The first topic on the **agenda** was **absenteeism**.*

Die schlechte Anwesenheitsstatistik des Fabrikpersonals hatte sich in den vergangenen Monaten zu einem weit verbreiteten Problem entwickelt.
Poor attendance among factory staff was becoming a common problem the last several months.

Aus meinen Jahren als Manager wusste ich,

31

dass Fehlzeiten von einer langen Liste von Gründen verursacht werden können.

I knew from years of being a manager that absenteeism could be caused by a long list of reasons.

Körperliche Erkrankungen oder Verletzungen, psychische Belastung und **Unzufriedenheit mit dem Beruf** waren nur einige von vielen Gründen.

*Physical sickness or injury, mental stress, **job dissatisfaction** were just a few of the many reasons.*

Als die Personalabteilung ihren Bericht vorlegte, wiesen ihre Gespräche mit den Arbeitern in der Fabrik auf ein größeres Problem hin, und es schien sich nicht spezifisch auf die Arbeiter, sondern ihre unmittelbaren Vorgesetzten zu konzentrieren.

When Human Resources made their report their discussions with front line workers on the floor indicated a bigger problem and it seemed to focus not specifically on the worker but on their immediate supervisors.

Die Arbeiter behaupteten, dass einige Vorgesetzte regelmäßig ihre Jobs und ihren Lebensunterhalt bedroht hatten, indem sie andeuteten, dass für viele ihrer **Stellenbeschreibungen Outsourcing** in Betracht gezogen wurde.

Workers claimed that some supervisors had routinely threatened their jobs and livelihood by suggesting that **outsourcing** *was being considered for many of their* **job descriptions.**

Sie hatten die Arbeiter auch gewarnt, dass die Einleitung zum Outsourcing ihrer Jobs eine **Zeitmanagement**-Studie war, die zu **Entlassungen** führen könnte.
They also warned workers that a prelude to outsourcing their jobs would be a **Time Management** *study which might translate into permanent* **layoffs.**

In Folge dieser Drohungen hatte es mindestens drei dokumentierte Auseinandersetzungen zwischen denselben beiden Vorgesetzten und mehreren Mitarbeitern gegeben.
As a result of these threats there had been at least three documented altercations between the same two supervisors and several staff members.

Die Auseinandersetzungen waren erhitzt gewesen und nicht physischer Natur, doch die Mitarbeiter waren erbost und nervös hervorgegangen.
The exchanges had been heated and were not physical in nature but had left staff members angry and nervous.

Die Wut und die **Unzufriedenheit der**

Mitarbeiter hatte sich schnell durch die Reihen ausgebreitet und eine direkte Barriere zwischen den Vorgesetzten und den anderen Arbeitern geschaffen.

The anger and **employee dissatisfaction** *had spread quickly through the ranks and created an immediate barrier between all the supervisory staff and the rank in file.*

Der örtliche **Betriebsrat**, der die Arbeiter repräsentierte, hatte bereits eine offizielle Beschwerde wegen **Schikane** eingereicht, doch leider erfuhr ich erst jetzt davon.

The local **shop steward** *representing the workers had already issued a formal complaint of* **harassment** *but, unfortunately, I was only learning about this now.*

Erschwerend kam noch hinzu, dass einer der Vorgesetzten angeblich ein rassistisches Schimpfwort gegen einen Maschienenführer verwendet hatte.

To make matters worse, one of the supervisors had allegedly used a racially derogatory term against a machine operator.

Nachdem ich von diesen Zwischenfällen gehört hatte, war meine erste Amtshandlung die Personalabteilung mit der **Lösung des Konflikts** zu beauftragen.

My first order of business, after hearing about

these incidents was to direct Human Resources personnel to begin the process of **conflict resolution.**

Das Unternehmen hatte nicht vor, bestehende Arbeitsplätze auszulagern, noch planten wir irgendwelche Zeitmanagement-Studien.
The company had no plans for outsourcing any of the existing jobs, nor were we planning any Time Management studies.

Die Drohungen der Vorgesetzten waren sinnlos und unprofessionell gewesen.
The threats from supervisors had been mindless and unprofessional.

Die rassistische Beleidigung durch einen Vertreter meines Management-Teams war vollkommen unverantwortlich und inakzeptabel gewesen.
The racial slur had been totally irresponsible and unacceptable coming from a representative of my management team.

Ich musste sicherstellen, dass alle, die bei Parker and Bowles arbeiteten, sich dessen bewusst waren.
I needed to ensure that everyone working at Parker and Bowles was aware of this.

Angesichts der **schäbigen Führungsfähigkeiten** die diese Vorgesetzten an den Tag gelegt hatten, bat ich die Personalabteilung ihre **Einstellungs**politik für das mittlere und obere Führungs**personal** zu überprüfen.

*Given the **shoddy leadership skills** shown by these supervisors I asked Human Resources to review their **recruitment** policies for middle and upper management **personnel**.*

Ich wies sie auch an, neue **Trainings**maßnahmen für beide dieser Gruppen einzuleiten.

*I also instructed that new **training** procedures be instituted for both these groups.*

Der Personalabteilung gegenüber betonte ich meine Erwartung, dass in Zukunft das gesamte Personal auf die entscheidende Bedeutung von **Diversität** und **Integration** aller Mitarbeiter am **Arbeitsplatz** hingewiesen wurde.

*I emphasised to Human Resources my expectation that in the future all staff be made aware of the vital importance of **diversity** and **inclusion** among all employees in the **workplace**.*

Als eine natürliche Anschlussmaßnahme zu den **Einstellungs- und Trainingsverfahren** führte ich ein neues Programm von **Leistungsbewertungen** ein, das regelmäßig alle sechs Monate sowohl für Arbeiter als auch für Management-Personal durchgeführt werden

sollte.
As a natural follow-up to **recruitment and training procedures** *I implemented a new program of* **performance appraisals** *that would be routinely scheduled every six months for both workers and management personnel.*

Als ich der **Sekretärin**, die von der Personalabteilung geschickt worden war, diese neuen Richtlinien diktierte, bemerkte ich ein Stirnrunzeln auf ihrem Gesicht.
As I was dictating these new directives to the **secretary** *sent from Human Resources I noticed a frown building in her face.*

„Habe ich irgendetwas übersehen?", fragte ich neugierig.
"Is there anything I missed?" I asked curiously.

„Sir, da gibt es in der Tat eine Sache", antwortete sie.
"Actually, Sir, there is one thing," she responded.

„Unter den Büroangestellten hat es in letzter Zeit viele Diskussionen über ihre Gehälter gegeben.
"There has been a great deal of talk among office staff lately about their wages.

Die Jungs in der Fabrik sind **gewerkschaftlich**

organisiert, doch wir sind es nicht
*The guys down on the floor are **unionized**, but we are not.*

Es scheint, als gäbe es innerhalb dieser Veränderungen Raum für einige ernsthaften Gespräche über die **Entgeltungleichheit**."
*It seems there might be some room in these changes for some serious talk about **wage disparity**."*

Ich lächelte. Sie hatte Recht.
I smiled. She was right.

Die **Gründungsmitglieder** dieses Unternehmens hatten eine große und wunderbare Idee gehabt.
*The **founding members** of this company had a great and wonderful idea.*

Die Idee steht an erster Stelle, doch direkt danach kommt die monumentale Aufgabe, sie umzusetzen.
The idea does come first, but after it follows the monumental task of making it happen.

Und dazu ist harte Arbeit nötig.
And that takes hard work.

„Wenn Sie wieder in ihr Büro kommen, bitten Sie Ihren **Abteilungsleiter**, zu mir zu kommen.
"When you get back to your office, ask your

department head to come and see me.

Ich werde nicht erwähnen, dass Sie Teil dieses Gesprächs waren", sagte ich.
I won't mention you were part of this conversation," I said.

Die Sekretärin lachte, als sie das Büro verließ.
The secretary laughed as she exited the office.

„Sie werden es nicht bereuen", rief sie über ihre Schulter.
"You won't regret it," she called over her shoulder.

„Ich weiß", lachte ich.
"I know," I laughed.

GERMAN

Anfangsschwierigkeiten

Ich bin am Montagmorgen früh aufgewacht, mit einem Knoten im Bauch so groß wie meine Faust. Wenn es einen Tag gab, der sich als der erste Tag vom Rest meines Lebens qualifizierte, dann war es dieser. Mein einziger Geschäftspartner und ich hatten später an diesem Tag einen Termin mit einem **Business Angel** um unseren **Businessplan** zu besprechen.

Ich saß am Fenster und für einen kurzen Moment blitzten mir tausend Dinge durch den Kopf. Doch wenn ich den nächsten Schritt machen wollte, musste ich mich konzentrieren. Ich nahm einen großen Schluck kalten Kaffee und wandte mich wieder der bevorstehenden Angelegenheit zu. Jedes Unternehmen, das etwas wert ist, beginnt mit einer Idee. Nach der Idee beginnt die harte Arbeit. Die harte Arbeit führt dann zu einem in sich geschlossenen Businessplan.

Mein Geschäftspartner Jim Bowles und ich hatten fast zwei Jahre lang an unserer Geschäftsidee gearbeitet. Wie viele unserer Generation waren wir mit einem gesunden Respekt vor der Umwelt aufgewachsen. Im

41

Licht unserer guten Erziehung und eines ausgesprochen sozialen Gewissens haben wir unsere Fähigkeiten und Energie zusammengerafft und sind in den Bereich der grünen Technologien vorgedrungen. Unsere Idee und Schwerpunkt waren Biokunststoffe. Mein Name ist Lannie Parker. Gemeinsam haben wir PARKER & BOWLES Bioplastics gegründet.

Biokunststoffe waren aus unserer Sicht mehr als nur eine trendige Offenbarung, die sich irgendein Umweltspinner ausgedacht hatte. Sie ergaben geschäftlich einen Sinn. Kunststoffe, als Baumaterial, hatten sich zu einem der wichtigsten Materialien in der **verarbeitenden Industrie** entwickelt. Weil Kunststoff ein Produkt auf Erdölbasis war, bedeutete das, dass ein großer Anteil der Unternehmenswelt, die Kunststoffe verwendet, vom Öl abhängig war; in Nordamerika und Europa bedeutete das oft, dass man von ausländischen **Exporten** abhängig war. Zu verändern, wie wir Kunststoffe herstellen und natürliches pflanzliches Material zu verwenden, um die Herstellung neu zu formulieren, würde eine Spielwende von monumentalen Ausmaßen bedeuten.

Mit Hilfe von Fetten und Stärken aus Pflanzen Kunststoff herzustellen würde eine ungesunde Abhängigkeit vom Öl beenden, die der Industrie helfen würde zahllose Dollars in der Herstellung zu sparen. Pflanzen zu benutzen um Kunststoffe herzustellen bedeutete, dass die Industrie sich vollkommen **erneuerbarer Ressourcen** bedienen konnte und dass das dazu führen würde, dass die Industrie das tun kann, was sie am liebsten tut... und das war Geld zu machen.

Unser Job heute war es, unseren **Business Angel** davon zu überzeugen, dass unsere Geschäftsidee vernünftig und tragfähig war. Unser **Businessplan** war die formelle Dokumentation unserer Geschäftsziele, wie sie erreichbar waren und der spezifischen Pläne, die wir anwenden wollten, um sie zu erreichen. Wenn wir unsere Hausaufgaben gemacht hatten, würde unsere Geschäftsidee die dringend benötigten Dollars unseres potentiellen Investors für uns gewinnen.

Als wir schließlich den **Business Angel** später an diesem Tag getroffen haben, waren wir überrascht, ihn zu kennen. Der Business Angel war ein ortsansässiger Geschäftsmann im Ruhestand, der im Alleingang zwei Baumärkte in der Region zu blühenden und erfolgreichen Unternehmen aufgebaut hatte. In der Tat so gut, dass ein riesiges Kaufhaus, das in der Region Einzug gehalten hatte, dem ortsansässigen Unternehmer klugerweise ein lukratives Angebot gemacht und sein Unternehmen aufgekauft hatte.
Als er anfing, unseren Businessplan durchzulesen, erinnerte er meinen Partner und

mich daran, dass jegliches Investment, das er in unser Unternehmen machen würde, im Austausch für **Wandelschuldverschreibungen** oder eine **Beteiligung am Eigenkapital** geschehen würde. Jim und ich sahen uns nervös an, während der ältere Herr seine Brille auf die Nasenspitze schob und mit ernster Miene weiter unsere Unterlagen überflog.

Die erste Komponente des Businessplans war die **Kurzfassung**. Was diesen Punkt anbelangte, fühlten wir uns sicher. Jim Bowles hatte in der Stadt in einer High-Tech Computer-Firma ein paar Jahre lang in einer Management-Funktion gearbeitet, bis das finanzielle Fiasko 2008 sie in den **Konkurs** getrieben hat. Sein eigentlicher akademischer Hintergrund war jedoch in der Chemie. Was mich betrifft, ich war der Betreiber/Eigentümer eines landwirtschaftlichen Zulieferunternehmens und hatte an der Uni im Hauptfach Betriebswirtschaft studiert.

Wir beobachteten, wie unser Business Angel mit dem Finger über das Papier zur nächsten Überschrift wanderte. Die war **Kundenanalyse**. Wir mussten beide im Stillen diesen Teil des Plans in unseren Köpfen durchgegangen sein, denn ein selbstbewusstes Lächeln machte sich auf unseren Gesichtern breit. Kunststoff war ein etablierter Baustoff. Wenn wir ihn billiger und umweltfreundlicher herstellen konnten als erdölbasierten Kunststoff indem wir ihn biologisch abbaubar machten, dann wäre er ein **Selbstläufer**. Alles würde auf einen guten, soliden **Umsatz** hinauslaufen.

Der letzte Teil des Businessplans war die **Wettbewerbsanalyse**. Welche Art von Unternehmen waren bereits auf dem Markt, die man als Wettbewerb betrachten konnte? Welche Fähigkeiten und Dienstleistungen unterschieden unser Unternehmen von den anderen und zeichneten uns in den Augen der **Verbraucher** aus? Angesichts der Art des Unternehmens und seiner grünen Technologie waren wir sicher, dass unsere Konkurrenz dünn gesät war. Es war eine relativ neue Technologie, und wir waren davon überzeugt in einen Markt einzutreten, der noch in den Kinderschuhen steckte. Es würde Kämpfe geben, doch mit Entschlossenheit hofften wird, uns den Hindernissen stellen und tragbare Lösungen für jedes vorstellbare Problem finden zu können.

Nach langer Überlegung sprach der Business Angel schließlich. Er war mit dem Lesen des Businessplans fertig. Er stellte alle relevanten Fragen. Seine Antwort war positiv. Er würde uns ein Investitionsangebot machen, unter der Voraussetzung einer **Due Diligence Prüfung**. Wir waren beide begeistert. Das war nur der erste Schritt, doch wir waren auf einem guten Weg. Ein Unternehmen war im Begriff, geboren zu werden.

Ergreifen des Marktes

Das Schild von Parker and Bowles Bioplastics sah beeindruckend aus, wie es sanft zwischen zwei großen Pfosten auf dem Rasen vor dem Fabrikkomplex schwang. Lannie Parker, einer der **Eigentümer**, die die Firma gegründet hatten, wartete an der Tür.

„Guten Morgen Frau Fletcher, freut mich, Sie an Bord zu haben", verkündete Herr Parker, als ich näher kam.
„Ich freue mich, hier zu sein", antwortete ich. Herr Parker schüttelte mir die Hand und lächelte.
„Jetzt beginnt der eigentliche Spaß", sagte er.

Ich nickte und hätte fast laut gekichert, bevor wir das Gebäude betraten. Seiner Bemerkung stimmte ich nur teilweise zu. Es würde Spaß machen, doch es wäre auch eine Herausforderung. Die **Vermarktung** einer Idee oder eines Produktes, vor allem, wenn es noch immer neu und von **potentiellen Kunden** ungetestet ist, kann beängstigend sein. Als **Marketing-Beraterin** bin ich von Parker and Bowles Bioplastics beauftragt worden, ihre **Bedürfnisse** in Bezug auf ihr neues Produkt zu bewerten. Ich würde einen Aktionsplan aus einer Marketing-Perspektive entwickeln und schließlich den Kunden meine Ergebnisse präsentieren. Hoffentlich würde ich das Meeting mit den zum Weitermachen erforderlichen Informationen verlassen.

Aus den ersten Gesprächen war bereits klar, dass wir zuerst an einem **B2B**-Marketing-Plan arbeiten würden. Wie bei jedem Plan würde unser erster Schritt sein, die **Vorgaben und Zielsetzungen** herauszuarbeiten und zu priorisieren. Diese zu definieren war der zentrale Punkt auf der Tagesordnung des heutigen Meetings. Ich hatte bereits mit dem Recherche-Prozess begonnen und mein Team hatte ein paar Ideen zusammengetragen, die schließlich zum Entwicklungsprozess der hochwichtigen **Marke der Firma** führen würde. Direkt im Anschluss an die Definition der Marke käme der ganze Prozess der Umsetzung erfolgreicher Strategien, um das Parker & Bowles Bioplastic Produkt in eine Reihe verschiedener Branchen einzuführen, von denen einige noch nicht einmal wussten, dass sie das, was diese Firma zu bieten hat, brauchten. Unser Marketing-Ansatz müsste eine große Bildungskomponente beinhalten.

Wir mussten unser **Zielpublikum** über den **Wert** informieren, den dieser innovative Biokunststoff mit sich bringt. Meine Arbeit war mir zugeteilt worden. Doch für heute war es wichtig, mit den Kunden zusammenzuarbeiten um all diese wichtigen Vorgaben und Zielsetzungen zu konkretisieren bevor wir irgendetwas in die Wege leiten konnten. Alle mussten der gleichen Meinung sein, um diese Marketingkampagne zu einem Erfolg zu machen.

Wir wussten dass es eines unserer aktuellen Top-Ziele für Parker and Bowles war, den **Marktanteil** des Unternehmens zu **erhöhen**. Vor zehn Jahren waren sie unsere Kunden geworden und wir hatten den ursprünglichen Marketing-Plan entwickelt. Wir sind definitiv ein Teil der Erfolgsgleichung des jungen **Start-up** Unternehmens gewesen, das von dem Hintergrund solider Wissenschaft, ein paar Business Angels sowie einer Menge Hoffnung und Gebete gestützt worden war.

Ich saß an meinem Schreibtisch, betrachtete die neusten Statistiken und lächelte. Wir hatten erfolgreich eine Krise überstanden und ich war stolz auf die Anstrengungen meines Teams. Es gab eine Reihe von neuen Firmen in der Biokunststoff-Branche, die Parker & Bowles dicht auf den Fersen waren und immer mehr traten in den bereits vollen Markt ein. Im letzten **Quartal** hatten wir erstmals einen **Rückgang des Marktanteils** erlebt und wir wussten, dass wir unsere Bemühungen intensivieren mussten, **neue Marktsegmente** zu erschließen.

Der gegenwärtige **CEO** bei Parker & Bowles ist

bekannt für seine Fähigkeit, über den Tellerrand hinauszublicken. Er versteht die Notwendigkeit von Innovation und hat viel in die Entwicklung mehrerer brandneuer Produkte investiert. Er hat auch mit seinem Team gearbeitet um die Modifikation einiger bereits entwickelter Produkte zu überwachen. Diese Maßnahmen haben das Unternehmen dafür aufgestellt, in einige neue Marktsegmente vorzudringen. In den vergangenen drei Monaten hatten wir die Möglichkeit, eng mit ihm zusammenzuarbeiten um **Vertriebskanäle** für diese neuen und modifizierten Biokunststoffprodukte zu eröffnen und unsere Bemühungen haben sich deutlich ausgezahlt.

Ich war besonders erfreut über einen der neuen **Broker** mit dem wir in Verbindung mit unserer neusten Marketing-Kampagne zusammengearbeitet hatten. Sie hatte viele Verbindungen in jenen Ländern, in denen die aktuelle Gesetzgebung die Unternehmen dazu zwang, sich zu bessern. Das bedeutete, dass sie alle auf biologisch abbaubare Verpackungen für ihre Produkte umstellten. Es ist ihr auch gelungen, Verbindungen herzustellen und der **Vermittler** zu sein, der notwendig war, um in diese neuen Märkte **einzudringen**.

Wir waren **noch nicht ganz außer Gefahr** und ich wusste, dass es einige neue Herausforderungen geben würde, doch heute fühlte ich mich optimistisch. Die Dinge lagen besser für Parker & Bowles als im vergangenen Quartal, und ich hatte guten Grund zu glauben, dass wir nächstes Jahr noch mehr Grund zum Feiern haben würden.

Das Geheimnis unseres Erfolges

Nachdem ich einige interne Berichte von unserer Fertigung gelesen hatte, war ich alles andere als optimistisch was die **Gewinne** im kommenden Jahr anging. Als **CEO** bei Parker and Bowles war ich besonders stolz auf meinen **innovativen Ansatz** in Bezug auf **Marketing-Strategien**. Ich hatte eine gute ortsansässige Firma beauftragt, die **Strategien umzusetzen**, und wenn man dem **Finanzbericht** vom letzten Jahr Glauben schenken durfte, dann hatte sich dieser Schritt als Erfolg erwiesen.

Doch es schien, dass meine Marketing-Strategien nicht ausreichten. Zahlen lügen nicht und der vorliegende Bericht zeigte, dass die Produktion im letzten Quartal deutlich gesunken war. Anhand der Daten, die ich von meinem Manager erhalten hatte, wusste ich sofort, dass das Problem unsere eigenen **Arbeitskräfte** waren. Der Rückgang der **Arbeitsproduktivität** musste gemeinsam mit den Abteilungsleitern der Produktion und dem **Personalmanagement** analysiert werden. Ich wollte, dass beide Abteilungen die vorliegenden Daten prüften und so viele Informationen wie möglich in der Fabrik sammelten. Sie mussten direkt an die Quelle gehen. Ohne direkten und ehrlichen Input von den Arbeitern selbst wäre jeder Bericht strittig und offensichtlich von zweifelhafter Aussagekraft.

Anfang der folgenden Woche traf ich mich mit den **Abteilungsleitern**, um die Ergebnisse ihres Berichts zu diskutieren. Unsere Arbeitskräfte bei Parker and Bowles setzten sich aus zwei Hauptgruppen zusammen. Da gibt es die Gruppe der Arbeiter in der Fabrik, die direkt mit unserem Produkt arbeiten, und dann gibt es unser Büropersonal. Es gibt auch noch eine dritte Gruppe, die in diese Diskussion miteinbezogen werden musste, nämlich die Manager. Es wäre interessant zu sehen, ob die Aufgabe, die ich meinen beiden Abteilungen gegeben habe, auch **Leistungsbewertungen** des Management-Bereichs beinhalten würde.

Der erste Punkt auf der **Tagesordnung** waren die **Fehlzeiten**. Die schlechte Anwesenheitsstatistik des Fabrikpersonals hatte sich in den vergangenen Monaten zu einem weit verbreiteten Problem entwickelt. Aus meinen Jahren als Manager wusste ich, dass Fehlzeiten von einer langen Liste von Gründen verursacht werden können. Körperliche Erkrankungen oder Verletzungen, psychische Belastung und **Unzufriedenheit mit dem Beruf** waren nur einige von vielen Gründen.

Als die Personalabteilung ihren Bericht vorlegte, wiesen ihre Gespräche mit den Arbeitern in der Fabrik auf ein größeres Problem hin, und es schien sich nicht spezifisch auf die Arbeiter, sondern ihre unmittelbaren Vorgesetzten zu konzentrieren. Die Arbeiter behaupteten, dass einige Vorgesetzte regelmäßig ihre Jobs und ihren Lebensunterhalt bedroht hatten, indem sie andeuteten, dass für viele ihrer **Stellenbeschreibungen Outsourcing** in Betracht gezogen wurde. Sie hatten die Arbeiter auch gewarnt, dass die Einleitung zum Outsourcing ihrer Jobs eine **Zeitmanagement-**Studie war, die zu **Entlassungen** führen könnte.

In Folge dieser Drohungen hatte es mindestens drei dokumentierte Auseinandersetzungen zwischen denselben beiden Vorgesetzten und mehreren Mitarbeitern gegeben. Die Auseinandersetzungen waren erhitzt gewesen und nicht physischer Natur, doch die Mitarbeiter waren erbost und nervös hervorgegangen. Die Wut und die **Unzufriedenheit der Mitarbeiter** hatte sich schnell durch die Reihen ausgebreitet und eine direkte Barriere zwischen den Vorgesetzten und den anderen Arbeitern geschaffen.

Der örtliche **Betriebsrat**, der die Arbeiter repräsentierte, hatte bereits eine offizielle

Beschwerde wegen **Schikane** eingereicht, doch leider erfuhr ich erst jetzt davon. Erschwerend kam noch hinzu, dass einer der Vorgesetzten angeblich ein rassistisches Schimpfwort gegen einen Maschienenführer verwendet hatte.

Nachdem ich von diesen Zwischenfällen gehört hatte, war meine erste Amtshandlung die Personalabteilung mit der **Lösung des Konflikts** zu beauftragen. Das Unternehmen hatte nicht vor, bestehende Arbeitsplätze auszulagern, noch planten wir irgendwelche Zeitmanagement-Studien. Die Drohungen der Vorgesetzten waren sinnlos und unprofessionell gewesen. Die rassistische Beleidigung durch einen Vertreter meines Management-Teams war vollkommen unverantwortlich und inakzeptabel gewesen. Ich musste sicherstellen, dass alle, die bei Parker and Bowles arbeiteten, sich dessen bewusst waren.

Angesichts der **schäbigen Führungsfähigkeiten** die diese Vorgesetzten an den Tag gelegt hatten, bat ich die Personalabteilung ihre **Einstellungs**politik für das mittlere und obere Führungs**personal** zu überprüfen. Ich wies sie auch an, neue **Trainings**maßnahmen für beide dieser Gruppen einzuleiten. Der Personalabteilung gegenüber betonte ich meine Erwartung, dass in Zukunft das gesamte Personal auf die entscheidende Bedeutung von **Diversität** und **Integration** aller Mitarbeiter am **Arbeitsplatz** hingewiesen wurde.

Als eine natürliche Anschlussmaßnahme zu den **Einstellungs- und Trainingsverfahren** führte ich ein neues Programm von **Leistungsbewertungen** ein, das regelmäßig alle sechs Monate sowohl für Arbeiter als auch für Management-Personal durchgeführt werden sollte.

Als ich der **Sekretärin**, die von der Personalabteilung geschickt worden war, diese neuen Richtlinien diktierte, bemerkte ich ein Stirnrunzeln auf ihrem Gesicht.

„Habe ich irgendetwas übersehen?", fragte ich neugierig.
„Sir, da gibt es in der Tat eine Sache", antwortete sie.

„Unter den Büroangestellten hat es in letzter Zeit viele Diskussionen über ihre Gehälter gegeben. Die Jungs in der Fabrik sind **gewerkschaftlich organisiert**, doch wir sind es nicht. Es scheint, als gäbe es innerhalb dieser Veränderungen Raum für einige ernsthaften Gespräche über die **Entgeltungleichheit**."

Ich lächelte. Sie hatte Recht. Die **Gründungsmitglieder** dieses Unternehmens hatten eine große und wunderbare Idee gehabt. Die Idee steht an erster Stelle, doch direkt danach kommt die monumentale Aufgabe, sie umzusetzen. Und dazu ist harte Arbeit nötig.

„Wenn Sie wieder in ihr Büro kommen, bitten Sie Ihren **Abteilungsleiter**, zu mir zu kommen. Ich werde nicht erwähnen, dass Sie Teil dieses Gesprächs waren", sagte ich.

Die Sekretärin lachte, als sie das Büro verließ. „Sie werden es nicht bereuen", rief sie über ihre Schulter.
„Ich weiß", lachte ich.

ENGLISH

Growing Pains

I woke up early Monday morning with a knot in my stomach as big as my fist. If any day in my life was going to qualify as the first day of the rest of my life, this would be it. My only business partner and I were scheduled to meet with an **angel investor** later in the day to discuss our **business plan**.

I sat at the window and for a brief moment a thousand things flashed through my mind. But if I was to **move to the next step** I needed to focus. I took a long drink of cold coffee and returned to the matter at hand. Any business **worth its salt** begins with an idea. After the idea, the hard work begins. The hard work then translates into a **tight cohesive business plan.**

My **business associate** Jim Bowles and I had worked on our business idea for almost two years. Like many of our generation we had grown up with a healthy respect for the environment. In light of our good upbringing and a decidedly **social conscience** we gathered our skills and energy and pushed forward into the field of green technology. Our idea and area of focus was Bioplastics. My name was Lannie Parker. Together we **founded** PARKER & BOWLES Bioplastics.

Bioplastics in our view was more than just a **trendy epiphany** imagined by some tree hugger. It made good **business sense**. Plastics, as a building material, had become one of the **primary materials** used in the **manufacturing sector**. Because plastic was a petroleum based product that meant a huge portion of the **entrepreneurial** world using plastics was dependent on oil; in North America and Europe that often meant relying on foreign **exports**. Changing how we made plastic and using natural plant based material to reformulate its manufacture would be a **game changer** of monumental proportions.

Using the fats and starches from plants to make plastic would end an unhealthy dependence on oil, which would help industry save countless manufacturing dollars. Using plants to make plastic meant industry would be **tapping into** a totally **renewable resource** and that would allow industry to do what it enjoys best … that was making money.

Our job today was to convince our **angel investor** that our business idea was both **sound and viable**. Our **business plan** would be a formal documentation of our business goals, how they were attainable and the specific plans we intended on using to reach them. If we had done our homework our business idea would attract the much-needed dollars from our **potential investor**.

When we finally met the **angel investor** later that day we were surprised to see that we recognised him. The angel investor was a local retired businessman who had singlehandedly built two building supply stores in the area into a **thriving** and successful **business venture**. So well, in fact, that a huge box store moving into the area had wisely made a **lucrative offer** to the local business owner and subsequently **bought him out**.

When he began to read through our business plan, he reminded my partner and I that any investments he might make in our company would be in exchange for **convertible debt** or **ownership equity.** Both Jim and I looked nervously at one another while the older gentleman propped his glasses on the tip of his nose and proceeded to scan our paperwork with a serious look on his face.

The first component of the business plan was the **Executive Summary**. We felt confident at this point. Jim Bowles had been involved in a high tech computer company in the city in a management capacity for a good number of years or at least until the **financial fiasco** of 2008 drove it into **bankruptcy.** His actual academic background though was as a chemist. As for myself, I had been the operator owner of an agricultural supply company and a business major while in university.

We watched as our angel investor ran his finger down the paper to the next heading. It was **Customer Analysis**. We both must have been silently reviewing that portion of the plan in our heads at the very same time because a confident smile filled our faces. Plastic was an **established** building material. If we could make it cheaper than petroleum based plastic and more environmentally friendly through biodegrading then it would be a **no brainer**. It would add up to good solid **revenue**.

The last portion of the business plan was the **Competitive Analysis.** What kind of businesses already existed in the marketplace that would be considered **competition**? What skills and services would make our company different and make us stand out in the eyes of **consumers.** Given the nature of the business and its green technology we felt confident our competitors were **few and far between**. It was a relatively new technology and we felt we were **entering the market** in its infancy. There would be struggles, but with determination we hoped we could face the obstacles and find solid solutions to any perceivable problem.

The angel investor finally spoke after a long deliberation. He had finished reading the business plan. He asked all the pertinent questions. His response was favourable. He would make us an offer of investment, but conditional on **due diligence**. We were both ecstatic. It was only the first step but we were well on our way. A business was about to be born.

Capturing the Market

The sign for Parker and Bowles Bioplastics looked impressive as it swung gently between two large posts on the front lawn of the factory complex. Lannie Parker, one of the **founding** owners, was waiting at the door.

"Good morning Ms. Fletcher, glad to have you onboard," announced Mr. Parker as I drew closer.
"I'm delighted to be here," I responded.
Mr. Parker exchanged a handshake and a smile.
"Now the real fun begins," he said.

I nodded and almost chuckled out loud before entering the building. I agreed only partially with his comment. It would be fun but it would also be a challenge. **Marketing** an idea or product, especially when it is still new and untested by **potential customers**, can be daunting. As a **marketing consultant**, I was hired by Parker and Bowles Bioplastics to assess their **needs** with respect to their new product. I would formulate a plan of action from a marketing perspective and eventually present my findings to the client. Hopefully I would leave this meeting with the information required to move forward. From initial discussions it was already clear that to begin with we would be working on a **B2B** marketing plan. Our first step, as with any plan would be to highlight and prioritise **goals and objectives**. Establishing them would be central on the agenda in today's meeting. I had already begun the research process and my team had been pounding out some ideas that would eventually lead into the process of developing the all-important **company brand.**

Hard on the heels of establishing the company brand would come the whole process of implementing successful strategies to introduce the Parker & Bowles bioplastic product to a number of different industry sectors; some of which haven't yet woken up to the fact that they need what this company has to offer. Our marketing approach would have to include a large educational component.
We needed to let our **target audience** know what **value** this innovative bioplastic could bring to their table. My work was cut out for me. But for today it was important to work with the client to nail down those all important goals and objectives before we could set anything in motion. Everyone would need to be on the same page to make this marketing campaign a success.

We knew that one of our current top objectives for Parker and Bowles was to **increase market**

share for this company. It had been ten years since they had become our client and we had developed that initial marketing plan. We had definitely been part of the success equation for what was once a fledgling **start-up** company backed by some solid science, a few angel investors plus a hope and a prayer.

I was sitting at my desk looking over the latest statistics and I was smiling. We had successfully navigated a crisis and I was proud of my team's effort. There were a number of new companies in the bioplastics industry nipping at the heels of Parker & Bowles and more were entering an already crowded market place all the time. Last **quarter** had seen **market share erosion** for the first time and we knew we had to step up our program for developing **new market segments**.

The current **CEO** at Parker & Bowles is known for his ability to think outside the box. He understands the need for innovation and has invested heavily in the development of several brand new products. As well, he has worked with his team to oversee the modification of some already developed products. These actions have positioned the company to move into some new market segments. Over the past three months we were able to work closely with him to open up **channels of distribution** for these new and modified bioplastic products and our efforts were clearly paying off.

I was particularly pleased with one of the new

brokers we were working with in conjunction with our latest marketing campaign. She had many connections in the countries where current legislation was forcing companies to clean up their act. That meant they were all switching to biodegradable packaging for their products. She was able to make connections and be the **intermediary** that was needed to **penetrate** these new markets.

We hadn't completed rounded the corner yet and I knew there would be some new challenges ahead, but for today I was feeling optimistic. Things were better for Parker & Bowles than they were last quarter and I had good reason to believe there would be even more reason to celebrate next year.

The Secret of our Success

After reading some internal reports prepared by our production department, I was suddenly feeling less than optimistic about **profits** this coming year. As **CEO** at Parker and Bowles I took a special pride in my **innovative approach** to **marketing strategies.** I had hired a good local firm to **implement strategies** and if last year's **financial report** was any indication the move had been a success.

But it appeared my marketing strategies were not enough. The numbers don't lie and the present report indicated production was substantially down in the last quarter. I knew instantly from the data provided by my manager that the problem was our own **labour force**. The decrease in **labour productivity** needed to be **analysed cooperatively** by the production department managers and by **Human Resources management.** I wanted both departments to look at the existing data and collect as much information from the actual factory floor. They needed to go directly to the source. Without direct and honest input from the workers themselves, any report would be moot and certainly discredited.

I met with **department heads** early the following week to discuss the findings of their report. Our labour force at Parker and Bowles is comprised of two main labour groups. There is the labour group on the factory floor that works directly with our product and then there is our office staff. There was also a third group that needed to be included in this discussion, namely, the managers. It would be interesting to see if the assigned task I gave my two departments would include **performance appraisals** of the management sector, as well.

The first topic on the **agenda** was **absenteeism**. Poor attendance among factory staff was becoming a common problem the last several months. I knew from years of being a manager that absenteeism could be caused by a long list of reasons. Physical sickness or injury, mental stress, **job dissatisfaction** were just a few of the many reasons.

When Human Resources made their report their discussions with front line workers on the floor indicated a bigger problem and it seemed to focus not specifically on the worker but on their immediate supervisors. Workers claimed that some supervisors had routinely threatened their jobs and livelihood by suggesting that **outsourcing** was being considered for many of their **job descriptions.** They also warned workers that a prelude to outsourcing their jobs would be a **Time Management** study which might translate into permanent **layoffs**.

As a result of these threats there had been at least three documented altercations between the same two supervisors and several staff members. The exchanges had been heated and were not physical in nature but had left staff members angry and nervous. The anger and **employee dissatisfaction** had spread quickly through the ranks and created an immediate barrier between all the supervisory staff and the rank in file.

The local **shop steward** representing the workers had already issued a formal complaint of **harassment** but, unfortunately, I was only learning about this now. To make matters worse, one of the supervisors had allegedly used a racially derogatory term against a machine operator.

My first order of business, after hearing about these incidents was to direct Human Resources personnel to begin the process of **conflict resolution.** The company had no plans for outsourcing any of the existing jobs, nor were we planning any Time Management studies. The threats from supervisors had been mindless and unprofessional. The racial slur had been totally irresponsible and unacceptable coming from a representative of my management team. I needed to ensure that everyone working at Parker and Bowles was aware of this.

Given the **shoddy leadership skills** shown by these supervisors I asked Human Resources to review their **recruitment** policies for middle and upper management **personnel**. I also instructed that new **training** procedures be instituted for both these groups. I emphasized to Human Resources my expectation that in the future all staff be made aware of the vital importance of **diversity** and **inclusion** among all employees in the **workplace**.

As a natural follow-up to **recruitment and training procedures** I implemented a new program of **performance appraisals** that would be routinely scheduled every six months for both workers and management personnel.

As I was dictating these new directives to the **secretary** sent from Human Resources I noticed a frown building in her face.

"Is there anything I missed?" I asked curiously.
"Actually, Sir, there is one thing," she responded.

"There has been a great deal of talk among office staff lately about their wages. The guys down on the floor are **unionized**, but we are not. It seems there might be some room in these changes for some serious talk about **wage disparity.**"

70

I smiled. She was right. The **founding members** of this company had a great and wonderful idea. The idea does come first, but after it follows the monumental task of making it happen. And that takes hard work.

"When you get back to your office, ask your **department head** to come and see me. I won't mention you were part of this conversation," I said.

The secretary laughed as she exited the office. "You won't regret it," she called over her shoulder.
"I know," I laughed.

Polyglot Planet Recommends:

Learn German - Bilingual Book
The Life of Cleopatra (German - English), from Bilinguals

Learn German - Bilingual Book
(German - English) The Adventures of Julius Caesar, from Bilinguals

Learn German - Bilingual Book
Vercingetorix vs Caesar - The Battle of Gaul, from Bilinguals
(German - English)

Other Books part of the Learn German Parallel Text Series:

Learn German - Parallel Text
Easy Stories

Learn German II: Parallel Text
Easy Stories (English - German)

Learn German III: Parallel Text
Short Stories (Intermediate Level)

Learn German IV: Parallel Text
Easy Stories

Business German - Parallel Text
Short Stories

Printed in Great Britain
by Amazon

55633534R00043